It's an honour to be somebody's
someone.

One Winter Walk

A MEMOIR WRITTEN BY

PRIYANKA YESODHARAN

INDIA • SINGAPORE • MALAYSIA

ISBN
Paperback 979-8-89588-975-6
Hardcase 979-8-89610-708-8

Dedicated to,

My beloved father, Yesodharan K.

Contents

Preface

The profound emotion of grief compels us to rearrange our lives. Grief can occur from different kinds of loss. When our loved one passes away, it shatters our life. There might be times in our lives when we feel like we will no longer see the daylight, like the bitterest winter freezing everything in its path. Grief acts as a reset for us, much like the earth in winter before it meets the next spring.

As both a psychologist and a person who still navigates through the paths of grief, I understand and accept life's cycle and its nature. I've been inspired by the grief stages of Dr Elisabeth Kubler Ross. This framework helped me with the basic insight during my postgraduate days.

Grief is not linear, not everybody might touch every stage of grief as it is a personal journey. As a psychologist, I had insight. But the insight wasn't sufficient. To navigate something profound like grief, we require human connections and reflection of life's nature. My loss did alter my existence but gradually I did find strength from my sorrows and resilience from my inner self. This book is an exploration of one of the coldest winters I have faced.

I often find myself reflecting on the fragility of life, and when I chose to confront my personal grief, I realised that the coldness shall also pass, some warmth would certainly return. Winter is not entirely gone, much like grief; I am sure cold waves shall keep coming.

I have seen frozen souls and half dead sunken eyes - to honour and respect all of our grieving journeys, I had decided to ink my thoughts. This book mainly focusses on one such winter walk. It's quite personal, but I have love to share and some paths to guide. The sorrows I still carry and I am working on it, as I said the cold waves revisit. The frostbitten wind has passed away, now there are some reflections left from the warmth I have found and I invite you all to walk with me, maybe when we connect, we shall meet the spring soon!

Life is full of uncertainties. We had no idea of how our yesterdays would pass and we still have no idea about our tomorrows. The only moment we hold onto is the present - and "that shall too pass"! Our emotions are full of complexities. Our brains are wired for attachments despite knowing the dichotomous nature of life and death. It's only the period in between, that makes life what it is. We are all spectators and performers at the same time. But what happens when one of our favourite performers leaves the stage without bidding a proper goodbye?

Life is full of uncertainties. It doesn't take much time to become a storyteller from a spectator. In fact, we aren't mere spectators but the chosen ones to sense and experience when life unfolds its layers. We aren't mere spectators but custodians of connections. The eyes have witnessed a lot, the ears heard them; what more can we do than carry their echoes, imprints and dreams?! The play has to go on while the stage is awaiting, and the spectator transforms into the storyteller to celebrate the departed ones, cherish the memories and share stories of love, pain and resilience!

Part I

Denial

Chapter 1

Frostbitten Echoed Numbness

I could fully understand the doctor's words. They pierced right into my ears, every word resonating with clarity. My body succumbed to the hardest words, while my mind was unwilling to yield. My hands turned cold, and my voice quivered. "Please tell me, should we take him to some other place?" My hopeful eyes searched for an answer. I heard the doctor clearly for the first time, but these were the hardest words I've ever heard in my life. How can I convince my mind, which clings to hope, despite the undeniable truth that has already happened—too late for a favourable response?

The doctor clearly caught in the conundrum torn between professional obligations and human compassion. I am sure he had done this before. He might have announced 100 deaths. Well, how would I know the range? "Please say something", my mother's voice broke. The immense pain in her voice was palpable. I didn't have to turn my face to feel the weight of her pain. The doctor somehow gathered the courage, deciding to be a part of his professional obligation and looked straight at us posing a blunt demeanour, "Take him back home," he said, "he is no more".

Our world stood still. I felt it crumbling again. The ache was familiar but this time, it hit harder. The second feeling of crumbling since the loss of one of my closest friends just months prior. My mother's legs might have weakened. I saw her holding onto things though walking towards my dad. She let out a loud cry unwilling to let go her partner to the clutches of mortality. She was talking, crying and begging him to wake up. It went on for some time. I stood still amidst the storm. "Is it actually happening?" I asked myself. Of course, he should have slipped into the deepest slumber or else he would have been the one holding her tight!

I did try informing two of our relatives from the hospital minutes later my father was announced that he was no more. But according to my mother, I should have been a bit more sensitive while sharing such news. She was right. I straightaway called them announcing my loss before the dawn broke. Maybe I was too numb to follow the cultural decorum while delivering the news. It certainly was not my thing.

The first person I had called was Shyam. He must have been devastated. Later, one of my cousins. I handed over the phone to my mother walking out of the room. I moved towards the unoccupied corner of the hospital. I screamed out my pain and took long deep breaths gathering courage to carry the pending procedures. We took Papa home to carry the rituals while I had to visit the hospital again to collect the death certificate.

The weight of accountability bears much greater than any profound loss. I learnt it in a harsh way. Though I volunteered to record a statement asserting that my father had no current insurance policies, I was asked to video tape it. Formal verifications and accountability matter in legal procedures. A few neighbours and my father's friends were right there; eyes being silent witnesses to my crushing reality. I let them video tape while taking my statement. I remained stoically robotic, detached from the weight of my words. "Will your relatives be coming?" somebody enquired. I looked at them cluelessly. "Do you have relatives here?" enquired another. I did not have the answers. I was unprepared. Every question out of syllabus reminds me of the pronounced gap between my heritage and reality.

Growing up here as a Mumbai Malayalee while my parents hailed from Kerala have made me question my family ties on multiple occasions. Despite being an aid to a lot of their close ones, some of them stayed distant until some monetary help was required; some, not all! It was a common tale as similar questions lingered from other Mumbai-Malayalee friends. It must be a mere coincidence, I sighed…But what if it was a shared reality?

I collected the death certificate from the hospital. Though the questions from the embodied panel felt overwhelming I somewhere understood it was the need of the hour for them. I was thankful for the fact that they were being helpful with the process. I would run to my father in such cases of uncertainty – where do I run to now? Imagine how much pain would I've endured to have videotaped informing my father's passing away and ensuring that he wasn't currently a part of any insurance policy! It felt like each word was keyed mechanically.

I reached home right after collecting my father's death certificate. My mother held my hands as gently as she could, making me sit next to my father's body. "Body", the first term I heard from somebody gathered over there that forced me to acknowledge the reality. It wasn't just a mere attempt to depersonalise someone who was a living entity until a few hours ago but the coldest words to be used! I silently sat next to my father while he lied there…still.

Chapter 2

Shoring Up Against the Frost

We were surrounded by known and unknown people, gazing directly into our souls. Some were trying to register the pain, while others were mere spectators. The phone rang incessantly. The voices were familiar to those of relatives, friends and acquaintances. Some unknown faces showed up, the juniors and staff who had come to pay a final respect to their chief engineer. Some emoted pain and condolences while some were still in disbelief. Some comforted us that they would pray while some had their words faltered with frozen condolences on lips.

Two of us throb with something we defy believing in. How could any of this be real? Am I slowly succumbing into accepting this or will someone wake me up? I look at my dad as he lies still. I wonder how many times I must call him until he wakes up. A part of my heart knows that's impossible while another wants to try. What if the Lord were to show some mercy?

I could hear murmurs discussing further rituals. Uncle Babu stepped in. He was one of the people I'd called informing the news. Uncle Babu and Papa's bond had years of connection; like that of siblings. Uncle Babu was mentored by my Papa, who though not a teacher by profession, possessed a wealth of knowledge and experience.

"We need to bathe the deceased", Uncle Babu broke. It's a part of the ritual – I recollect. I was in grade 6th back then, while my grandma had passed away; I was told that the bathing the deceased is to show respect, moreover a part of purification to set for their afterlife. I stood up walking towards the bedroom, while my mom followed me to pick one of Papa's best clothes before she let him go for his afterlife.

Her hands ran through almost all of his clothes; she was particularly selective; she knew these garments would be his last. The clothes must have weighed more than the usual; my mom chose them with utmost reverence to honour him!

Mom insisted on bathing him. Uncle Babu strongly objected. He tried requesting initially but then it was of no help until he finally asserted, "I know he is your partner, but he is like my big brother to me. Let me take care of the rest please"! Mom agreed. Uncle Babu along with two other best friends of my Papa moved towards my Papa taking the garments from my mom.

They bathed, dressed and adorned him. My mother applied the 'Vibhuti'; holy ash on his forehead. It signifies a lot of things in our culture. Ashes are beyond purifications. I remember reading about how ashes looked like clusters of stars or some piece of the universe under a microscope. Maybe just like the wise says, "we return to wherever we come from"! Ashes are beyond physicality, a powerful reminder of what we leave behind.

One of my best friends Neha showed up with her family. She was unprepared but somehow was destined and entitled to perform a ritual with me. Neha initially came into my life as a stranger who chose to be my roommate during my undergrad days. We were of different ages, different courses but one thing was common; sisterhood. When she did a ritual with me, I started seeking answers. I wonder if she truly means beyond any bond that's not visible to my naked eyes.

One by one the rituals were performed in a structured manner. Each ritual carried the weight of a rock on my heart's weighing scale. With every rock being placed, the weighing scale drifts, numb with grief, lifting the other side into the shallow nothingness.

I looked at his tied toes remembering how a few days ago we had a conversation of how fascinating it is that I have gotten feet that totally resembled his. I leaned to kiss his forehead. My mind silently battled the cold sensation I felt on his forehead. It wasn't just the absence of warmth but an unsettling realisation that he is gone forever.

The kind people surrounded me all set to take dad's body to the cremation ground. Two souls with sunken eyes wandered silently asking for some more time but for how long? Me and mom knew that it was time to bid the last goodbye. My mom caressed my dad one last time, kissing on his forehead.

All the laughter, sorrow, conversations and moments we had shared only would exist in our memories. I understand we all are mortals but how could the essence and entity drain out completely and unexpectedly? Where did the warmth go?

"I have never seen my father lie this silent, this still!

His eyes were closed, motionless unlike while generally asleep.

What if in some time he wakes up for a glass of water?

Maybe I should be the one getting it.

He usually would wake up without alarms, that's how routined his body was.

Oh! I guess somebody here did mention his 'body'.

He seems like he's almost asleep, but this time no snores, no 'twitch'.

Looks like I was partially right, he slipped into slumber, really deep…"

They carried my dad for further rituals. My mind registered the ones who were here to pay the final respect. Some of my dad's staff shared moments they had the day before. Some shared the sweet memories of how kind and helpful my dad was. There were stories filled with love and compassion. Some expressed their disbelief. Some remained silent with teary eyes. Their presence felt powerful. I knew at least for some hours; we would have company. Eventually, the grief journey will primarily be for me and mom.

My aunt and cousin flew in from Kerala, crossing miles to be with us in our time of need. Their presence was reassuring. The adjacent wing neighbours fed us. It was difficult to get that started but they took responsibility to conquer us with love. It takes love to sustain during the darkest times. There were unannounced visits that kept coming even beyond the circles we knew. Everything that happened around was uncalled for. Maybe I should be facing the truth.

I tried consoling myself. I pondered over the plight of those who are still unwilling to settle in. The most recent painful transition might have been for the family members who had lost their loved ones to the pandemic. The pandemic in and itself left many with a dismal outlook setting a chain of depressed lives and emptiness. Some never might have gotten a chance to see the bodies, a final glimpse to set the realisation on! Fate being so merciless, the emotions might have been raw and unsettling.

However uncertain or unexpected anybody's death may be, the mind often grapples with the material possessions left behind. There might have been mothers struggling to let go of the little toys, a partner clinging onto their loved ones' clothes unable to let go of the fading scent, a sibling unwilling to take up the other part of the room leaving it on a permanent state of equilibrium, friends hesitant to delete the contact numbers even though the calls would be left unattended. The loved ones losing not just the person but a part of themselves left alone with bittersweet reminders, echoed promises and bland Sundays!

Chapter 3

A 'May' Cold Numbness

May 2021 was when I first learnt that fate can be mercilessly unpredictable. Almost 30 days of delusional clear skies and perfect nights. The only little thing that bothered me was the unattended calls of my friend. Maybe his phone broke? Maybe he's busy? I reassured myself. A few days ago, he asked if I could help him with something I usually assist him with – specifically, some support with practice sessions for one of his upcoming tests. I had helped him twice before, but this time I was caught up with my own examinations and viva. I had asked for some extra time. I wondered if me turning him down might have motivated him to avoid my calls.

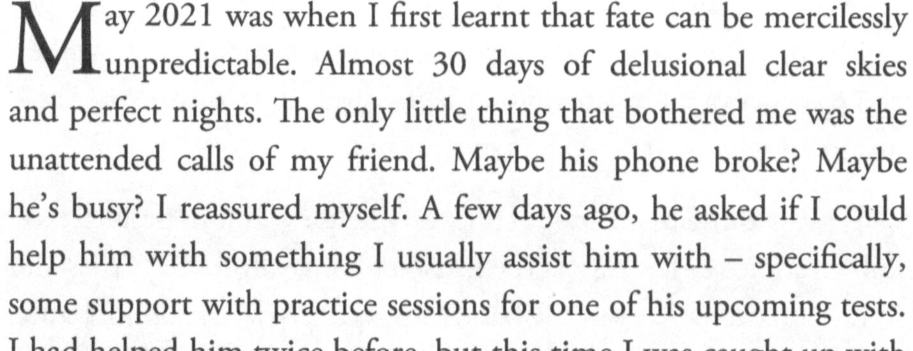

But no, that might have not been him. He was that person who was unaware of 'entanglements', silences never comforted him, fights would make him restless. He was the first man in my life to show me that a man can be gentle and coaxing, willing to mend things and hearts. I sent him messages expecting delayed responses like he did in the past. I was all at sword waiting to fight like last time we did because this time he pushed it too far and made me wait too long. A few days later, his absence started bothering me. I vented it out to Jyoti, my soul sister. Few minutes later, she sent me messages and screenshots of his Facebook pages where people had posted condolences over his death.

The earth beneath shattered. All this time, I waited to fight with someone who wasn't even alive?! I could barely stand up from my bed. I could barely breathe. I called her, crying and begging her to wake me up from the nightmare. She couldn't. The unpredictability of life had already consumed me. He was no more, covid took him away!

My parents rushed into my room to see me screaming. I hugged my mom tight, barely saying that my dearest friend, my brother, had passed away. I saw my father being speechless for the first time, unsure of what words would comfort me.

That was the first time I felt utterly helpless and in pain to have known someone left earth. The loss shook my world. Days passed. I found it hard to do even the basic things. Everyday an uphill battle. He was one of the few people who knew about my love relationship. I trusted him, he trusted me. I was 5 years younger than him, but we hardly noticed the difference because our bond felt ageless. Now, I am left with his hopes, dreams, a list of favourites, stories of his personal trauma, and peculiar patterns to identify some shades of his soul in some people; maybe in the coming lives...

It was hard for Jyoti too. She was the only witness to see our friendship bloom, and it was her who watched its lively graph fall drop dead. She never seemed exhausted while holding me from the miles she could. Whether it was 4:00 p.m. or 2:00 a.m., she remained my constant listener because she knew that for me it was a numbing pain.

I still remember, he would open up about his vulnerabilities, allowing me to soothe some of his darkest fears and troubles…as I said, he trusted me. Often, he used to discuss his pain and about wanting a less painful existence…

"Vi, where did you go?"

Lifeless echoes of familiar voices.

Past narratives and future dreams.

Why did we even share those?

If life was this less and no more,

Why did I even meet a kindred soul?

Maybe the world was too broken, it couldn't restore your light.

But what do I do with the pieces of your soul,

that's deep in my bones though out of sight?

Part II

Anger?

Chapter 4

Broken Icy Tapes

I remember running a floor down in disbelief when they carried my dad for further rituals. Neha rushed along stopping me. I hugged her, releasing all my gathered-up strength as I grew weaker and nearly succumbed.

"Heard that you had recently got a job. Sad that your father passed away", stated one of our meddlesome aunts; precisely one of the apartment residents. My eyes turned towards her wondering what words she would throw next. "Would your pay be enough to cover the family expenses? How much are you offered?"

Her words sounded just like that of a genuine well-wisher. I never knew Mrs Meddlesome would put this 'genuine concern' out there during this very ideal moment. Discussing finances with someone who just lost their dad is definitely a wonderful choice! My cold eyes fixated on her, recalling every contemptuous moment I ever had with her. Within seconds I could see her hesitating, reassuring me of how insensitivity was masked behind her false sympathy.

Her insensitivity was nothing new to me. That's exactly why I kept stepping away from her despite knowing her for more than a decade. My heavy heart yearned for a hug but I was certain that no matter what, I wouldn't go to her pretentious arms. Despite being broken, I was particular about whom I sought for some solace. I did wait for Neha's mother to show up for some solace. I don't know if my feelings were valid at that point of time but it still surprises me how insensitive people can be.

One of my childhood friends had also come with their family. The hugs were warm. The affection was genuine. I had known them for more than a decade too but this familiarity was comforting. It wasn't about the familiarity but the affection. The comfort of knowing no matter how miles far we go, the affection remains unchanged.

We seek solace from familiar faces; especially when lonely in an unfathomable labyrinth. Some of my closest friends couldn't make it to the funeral. They had their reasons. Some were held back by illness while some singled out stating about the uncertainty and being unaware of how to comfort me. Maybe my need for solidarity outran personal and logistical reasons. Would it have been the same if I were close kin of theirs? The isolation hit hard.

Maybe it's some new challenge for me and my mom to grapple with the labyrinth. Maybe anger wasn't a valid emotion? I mean, we all have personal experiences with grief. Maybe anger was just a mask and deep down it was a feeling of helplessness. I felt like I needed to maintain a sense of control. My mind almost turned into a tumultuous sea, unwilling to surrender to its vulnerability. I called up Shyam to let him know that it was okay if he couldn't show up. I remember I had asked if he could make it. I had even assured that it would be okay if he couldn't.

"I had to confess our relationship to my parents, I'm coming to your place," said Shyam. The tumultuous sea swiftly settled into absolute stillness. It was a big move for us. His parents knew me, but not in this way. His elder sister and I were friends but me and Shyam could never acknowledge our bond openly.

Due to personal reasons, I couldn't reveal that I was in a relationship with him. It wasn't just a personal decision but more of social expectations that drove us on the complexities. As adults, we both had the right to keep certain decisions private as per circumstances; I wouldn't have emphasised this point if a lot of people had an understanding of respecting individual decisions. A bond that was meant to be shared during one of our happiest times shattered, as if some uninvited clown disrupted it in the most tragic way!

When Shyam chose to break all barriers, despite the strong reasons we had, it was a bold move on his part. He did it for me. His gesture touched me in ways like nobody did. I did not insist but the level of unspoken understanding stood out. This single gesture conveyed more than any words could. The tints of hopelessness slowly felt like fading away. A pinch of hope soothed my wounds. The impression kept lingering.

Imagine being scrutinised for not letting someone know about something really private in our lives. This happened barely months after my dad's passing away. A close acquaintance of ours visited home on the pretext of sharing condolences but ended up having almost a 30-minute interrogation session. They wanted to know about why I had kept my love life private. A valid question deserves an answer (maybe not all questions) but was it a right time to discuss all of this? Their question cloaked a façade of concern hardly affecting any of their lives. Maybe they're just curious? Maybe they deserve to know?

It was our mutual decision to keep our commitment private; not secret. We had our reasons. I chose to let them know one of the reasons. Shyam was not settled and was still seeking a job, a fair reason that most would understand. Society mostly has ridiculed men who have found a partner but are struggling for stable employment. I had agreed to keep our relationship private as I've seen his earnest efforts already being overshadowed by stigma. I've observed that someone who is in their temporary struggling phase might deal with judgemental glances making them question their very own existence! To some, the treatment of society and audacity might leave them with permanent scars. The probing comes out of nowhere as if every single question deserves an answer rightfully!

I understand how beliefs of gender roles have been deeply ingrained since ages. Some men struggling to provide being seen as economic failures, some women who could do all of them yet being trivialised. These rigid expectations paved its way across generations. I've personally seen the societal pressure upon these struggling men – their mind is always at war! They lock up their tears behind some imaginary iron bars crowned by society's vultures who circle around their lives waiting for the perfect moment to pounce upon their struggles.

Considering all of these we had an understanding. We sought privacy and waited for the perfect moment to share the news only to realise that it never existed. Some of our friends knew, it felt a bit safer contemplating less or no judgement. We had also mutually decided on letting my mom know this. I've always found it difficult to keep it hidden from her. Maybe I am bad at lying, maybe moms have in-built lie detectors. I made sure that dad was familiar with Shyam's name, though I never had a chance to confess this. I often mentioned Shyam during our regular conversations. Maybe, little by little I was trying to make things more apparent!

Well, these were the honest reasons I had given them. Despite not owing an explanation I decided to share a private piece of our lives considering respect and courtesy. The frustration and dissatisfaction reflected on their faces. How could they expect me to inform them of something that has never even been discussed with my own dad? She then moved on to lecturing me about values that I could assure were rather 'ironical'. Thanks to that day, I was shown how self-centred a person could be, especially in front of a widowed mother with welled up eyes in memories of her husband. To me, not shedding a single tear wasn't much difficult as I was taken aback by her level of insensitivity.

The way of interrogation lacked affection, sensitivity and respect. My answers might have not soothed their preconceived notions, rehearsed 'prose' and taped responses. Without making much of an eye contact, she rose briskly to leave. The room felt relieved as soon as she left but the air inside felt ruthless hovering around her remarks!

I did recollect other situations which may or may not reflect insensitivity. I remember one of my friends sending me pictures of some dessert she was savouring on right after we left a bereaved home. It was some unplanned celebration which could have been done without. I wasn't even sure if I was in a place to judge or even question someone else's personal choices but something felt unsettling. Hardly 45 minutes ago we were at Missie's home where we condoled with her on the loss of her father.

The sudden switch felt odd, since she was closer to Missie. The melancholy of silent whispers and glimpses of her deceased father remained vivid in our minds. The perfectly plated pictures of delights ironically felt unappealing! How could she remain unaffected by any of these or did grief forget to get deep in her bones since that was a personal suffering?

But who am I to measure those complexities of human nature? I am wondering if her actions were driven by her way of grappling grief? Perhaps her choices serve as a coping mechanism. What entitles me to judge? Through the lens of grief, the nuanced emotions in the bigger picture are expertly blended, making them hard to discern.

"The mirror of the world broke in two pieces,

And I might have stepped onto some very wrong.

I let that consume me out of hurt.

Unkind shadows followed, but disguised masks fell off.

Stirring rage out of my pain.

To have witnessed fractured thoughts,

To have smelled twisted ideas,

To have felt broken hearts -

The daggered blows and parched throats did always help.

It reminded me that I must speak,

Unwilling my sorrow to bleed,

Unwilling to surrender,

And to hold on to the right pieces,

Creating the graffiti I needed."

Chapter 5

Snowbound Impasse

I just recalled another incident that struck me this past May. My mom let me in on some details about someone she was familiar with. It was a story of a step-mother. To dive deep into the bare bones, months of mistreatment by the step-mother despite the distance wasn't just it. The lady tore off the entitlements of the legal wife and their daughter.

The daughter, who was shunned away from the family, visited her paternal grandmother to bid final goodbyes. Her young hands trembled as she held her grandmother's cold wrinkled still hands for one last time. The relief of meeting her father after months, but the heaviness of her grandmother's death, could have been a personal disarray of her emotions' battleground. The daughter sensed her step-mother's cold gaze from a distance. "Have you come to stake your part of the claims?" the words spat out of her step-mother's mouth. A barrage of questions and accusations flooded, as if pre-prepared.

The daughter had no expectations of mercy from a woman who was devoid of any affection. The words of her step mother might have taught her to heap scorn while she was only 12, when her step mother reflected on her insensitive thought of legacies and familial disputes.

She looked at her dad with pity; it was a dead end. The assets? The property? The legacy? The stepmother spat words accusing the daughter of some non-existent greed. The daughter left, but the shrewdness of her step-mother continued. Perhaps she never experienced a pang of conscience!

With more of a keen observation, I realised this wasn't just a single lapse of empathy but rather a broken tape of recurring indifference. Why would humans intentionally do that? It would be a presumption to say that only humans process grief intricately unlike other animals. But being somewhat advanced how could some of us remain this unaffected? The patterns evoke a part of society's indifference to human suffering. Where do they go descending far from the steps of a compassionate society?

Chapter 6

Seeking Answers in Icy Waters

My anger towards God consumed me. It fuelled up with memories of every dealing which felt unjust with higher executions! When covid took my 29-year-old friend who was bereft of enough worldly experiences, I needed answers. When dad passed away with unfulfilled dreams, probably the one which he yearned for, I was mad at God. My dad felt like a reminiscent of his mother who had left while my dad was still young. Well, at least he was blessed with some time with her. The most unjust thing he had to face was when his father passed away a day before some festival, while he was only 3 or 4 years old. Life was hard for both my parents. But thinking of my dad, to have lost his father so young might have been the worst betrayal. I have heard that pain is inevitable but suffering is a choice - so who gets to decide? The bearer, the provider or the so-called transactions one might be still deciphering?

For my dad, his mother was the only aid during his younger times. He would often talk about her sacrifices and her valour. Maybe it was her prayers that brought him to Bombay - the city of dreams. She had definitely reassured him that things are going to fall into the right places from halfway across the country. Bombay (as called back in the mid-80s) gave him new beginnings. His story was truly exemplary. To recall it from the hazy dream would be like the pieces of little pictures without the complete collage. I remember stories of him telling me how he would work all day and study during the night. Unyielding determination and perseverance made him what he was! My mom had her story of strength and resilience too. She is the strongest woman I have ever known. Sadly, she buried much of her trauma in silence, as she was uncomfortable sharing with others. She didn't deserve to carry such a heavy burden alone. If I could only go back in time with a time machine and hold her the way she truly needed it! Their generation had it so tough. For me, these narratives weren't just resilient stories but relentless struggles.

If you ask me, my dad who had such struggles deserved a better farewell. Death could have been a bit kinder, slowly guiding his wrinkled hands, caressing his grey head with comfort of his loved ones besides on a peaceful summer day. For the friend whom I had lost, the 29-year-old man was carried away towards the afterlife, maybe he felt homesick, unsure if earth was where we all belonged?! How about the toddlers? The ones who lost it to the wars? The children? I needed answers but being a negligible creation in this vast universe, the answers would have been beyond what any of us could perceive, I knew that.

Lingering on these thoughts, I realised that their life wasn't a rocking chair. Grief felt like a whirlwind of emotions ending up in the same place of anger; deep beneath lies melancholy. The thoughts shifted from their plight to mine. My pain wasn't that excruciating when I compared to theirs but it was different. My pain was valid though! If I don't reveal every personal part of pain in here, it doesn't mean I never had any. I had my share of melancholic, sunken days when outcasts would expertly cover my part of summer making it unnoticeable to others. It remains in the silence of the slumber in the deepest corners of my mind. Maybe, this wasn't the right time…

I battled not knowing where the anger was rooted from. Was it because I felt injustice by some unknown power and its uncanny patterns? Was it because I was selfish about their existence and how much I identified with them? I wanted to introspect my own motivations. My fingers strived to point at someone, anyone who was responsible, but they never knew where or when to point. Guess what? I will never find that, no one will ever.

"Empty vessels, no pickled jars;

No gentle hands to soothe,

No bedtime stories.

Before I could gather their hugs and laughter,

Death had swept them away - my grandparents.

I was bereft of their warmth.

I did not know how it felt to have a sibling.

I did not spend much moments with closed blooded cousin ties.

My pet was taken away by death when I was 9.

I felt angry and futile.

But again, why was I angry?

And why long for the attachments unmade?

Moreover, to whom I was angry at?

What if it's my own misdeed from some unseen past holy ledgers?

Maybe I should bargain with fate to lessen the agonies;

That might set my caged rage free."

Part III

Bargaining

Chapter 7

Amplification

The night preceding the tragic incident was unlike the regular one. We didn't have the slightest notion of what was about to happen. That night, I experienced feelings of fear and uncertainty slowly settling into kindling into hopes of a future rich with blessings.

Dad and Mom sat on the bed placed next to my work chair. I immersed myself in work, not out of dedication to my new job but seeking a momentary escape from Dad's questions. Dad seemed happier than usual, perhaps because Mom had already told him about Shyam. Maybe he was relieved to have dodged the typical Indian groom hunt, or the fact that he was already familiar with Shyam.

Dad kept trying to make small talk, and though I responded, it was half-hearted. At any moment then, he might have started asking more about the relationship. He was warm but my heart pounded with anxiety. I could feel my cheek flush. I wasn't prepared for this. Thoughts overpowered my emotions. "Would he still see me as his little girl?" The question might have stemmed from a deep-seated fear of transition. I wasn't prepared to discuss the relationship but I was willing to answer if questioned. I was finding it hard to navigate my emotions.

In India, the prospect of a father learning about their daughter's relationship could alter the situation in whatsoever direction. I suppose this fear has been deeply rooted in the minds of the majority of daughters. We had conversations about my work life. I was finding it a bit difficult to maintain eye contact with dad but the times I could, I did notice an unusual spark of curiosity and excitement.

After some time, dad moved to the next room to listen to his bedtime playlist. He left with a smile on his face with anticipation of happy revelations.

As soon as dad left the room, I was in the midst of discussing things with Shyam. Shyam's anxiety was justified yet he promised to speak with my father first thing in the morning. I felt a deep sense of shared responsibility. Whatever the outcome may have been, we were both equally invested.

Dad knocked on my door. It was time for him to snuggle into bed. He waved me his usual 'snug as a warm cotton ball' goodnight. There was unprecedented content on his face. Dad retired to his bed. I texted Shyam of the happenings. Both of us had a deep sense of relief to see that dad was happier on learning about the relationship. The weight fell off our shoulders now that decision was made that we shall have the conversation with dad in the morning. We too drifted off to sleep.

Everything felt as though it was about to fall into places perfectly. Behind the veil of unforeseen happiness, death lurked in the shadows, clutching onto its laughter, poised to make an unexpected entrance and ambush every single seed of joy!

Some hours later, I was jolted awake. Something felt wrong. Mom was in a state of panic desperately trying to convey something. I was momentarily disoriented as I woke up from deep sleep.

"Dad had called, asking if we could quickly make it to the ground floor", mom hurried up.

Chapter 8

Surge

We sprinted as quickly as we could. Fear and uncertainty seeped into my bones. My hands felt cold, my chest pounded and legs trembled. Upon reaching I saw my father struggling to breathe. The plain sight of him gasping felt colder than the coldest of January mornings I was experiencing. My dad barely could speak, he sensed death and he confided the same to mom. My mom rushed to his side, hands caressing his back and reassuring. She reached out to his shirt's pocket and took out the car key to rush him to the hospital. Dad had a regular routine of driving his car early in the morning. Fate didn't let him have his daily routine. She tried carrying and guiding him towards our car but failed.

"Call the neighbour," her voice urged with panic. Within minutes the neighbours arrived. They managed to help dad get into the backseat. I sat beside my dad. Mom took the wheel; her hands gripped the steering with unusual determination. The neighbour almost as old as my dad co-ordinated by glancing back to check on dad. Mom sped up navigating through the coldest winds of uncertainty. It was around 5:30 in the morning with only the faintest hint of dawn on the horizon.

My hand cradled dad in a tender embrace while he battled to breathe. I could feel his cold sweat. His eyes spoke helplessness. I gently reassured that everything was going to be alright. His gaze suggested a silent plea that wanted to say something. I knew fate was being unkind but I comforted him with reassurances and caresses filled with affection as I could sense mortality. I was unsure if my words could overpower his fears.

I tenderly kissed his forehead with all the love and strength I could gather. It wasn't merely a kiss but a silent testament honouring him for the bond we shared. The kiss wouldn't have paid justice but would have imprinted the love of his daughter deeper in his soul. I wished my message crossed through the fading light of his consciousness that he had been the best father I could have ever hoped for. He looked into my eyes and I saw the most haunting juxtaposition; a poignant blend of love and death.

The sound of the morning streets was more audible with the deafening stillness inside our car. We reached the hospital and the neighbour rushed with the stretcher. They carried him into the emergency unit while he was no more!

Everything fell into the right places a few hours ago. And then, it felt like I crossed over some invisible door like a parallel universe overlapped just making me question my ground beneath. Here, in this world all the details looked the same but the essence - unfamiliar!

Did I sign up to endure this pain? Where exactly did the higher powers thought I would find the light to endure and hold this weight of unimaginable pain? Who would the almighty have trusted me with this blind darkness? I was unsure with whom I was wrestling for my fate but I needed answers.

Monotonous mornings fill in the bland

Until a stormy dawn strikes unplanned.

With what hope do we go to sleep?

With hope that cold will slowly creep?!

Death, sometimes scarcely visible and knows no ties.

I knew it when the daughter in me, saw death in my father's eyes.

Unspoken words and his soul unbound.

Made me walk through a fragile ground.

Lunatically seeking a monotonous morning from the past.

To set myself free from the gravity of what I've lost.

Chapter 9

The Ceremony

We revolve around an array of speculations about where the soul goes after death. The beliefs that prevail differ among communities. Where? The question would continue to remain as a question to us; the mortals, haunting us. But whatever and however our rituals vary in countless ways, we all seek the same goal; peace. To remain an embodiment or remnants of the ones we loved must be an honour.

The post death rituals signify decades of dedication as an ode to our loved ones. Grief, as we know, is an immense and profound thing to experience. There is no correct way to grieve, but a set of rituals drawn about from the ancient scriptures definitely helps us navigate through the grief journey. It is a compass towards acceptance for the unsettling minds where the wise have carved out and perfected on. Most of us lack insight during such unprecedented times and I personally have felt these rituals have helped me with a structure to deal with intense emotions.

When I said we all seek the same goal, it was for both the parties: the departed ones and the survivors. For the survivors, it is to pay homage to the departed ones. For the departed ones, it is liberation. As mentioned before, we all have different versions of stories to it, every story has a common climax - peace that comes with acceptance. If nothingness would be an answer to some, could I infer that they are still stuck at some stage of grief?

We (mom, me and my cousin brother) had offered honour to my deceased dad by conducting Shradh (paying homage to the departed ones). It was one of the coldest January mornings. In our car, there were five of them. My mom was in her driving seat, seated beside my fiancé Shyam. Me, my aunt and my cousin-brother in the backseat. Another car had my dad's friends. One of our neighbours took accountability waiting near the cremation ground with an urn carrying my dad's holy ashes. We were to collect it on our way to the river side where the Shradh was supposed to be performed. The car stopped to collect the urn.

My father who had dreamed of walking me down the aisle and giving my hand to the groom, has silently embarked on an infinite journey. The groom who had dreamed of receiving his fiancé's hand from her father's hands, now holds the urn bearing the weight of unspoken blessings. The sole thought of it felt gut wrenching. The world felt meaningless and unfair.

We reached the riverbank. We were not the only ones. There were other sunken eyes too. Some with single parents, some where their child left soon, to some it was a young adult who had unfulfilled dreams. The grief filled air competed with the coldest breezes of January for the ones who had bathed in the river as a part of ritual. There were a set of rituals structurally performed under a mentor. These weren't merely rituals but the wisdom reflected from various sources over countless centuries. We seek forgiveness for the mistakes we have knowingly-unknowingly caused to the deceased and the ancestors. We pray for their afterlife journeys to be a smooth sail. We symbolically believe that the souls arrive, witness the love we offer through such acts and then leave, forgiving our mistakes and blessing us to face the world.

I felt much lighter after performing the rituals. Some sort of realisation passed over that maybe our time here might be temporary but the love is not. When I prayed for my father and the ancestors whom I have never met in my course of life; it felt like an acknowledgement. A renewed sense of connection welcomed me when I finally rose from the coldest waters of the river after the rituals. A mixed set of feelings kept on reflecting although some of the unresolved feelings waved a goodbye. I knew it was a beginning towards the step of acceptance of his loss when physically I had performed the rituals. A partial sense of closure bloomed in.

Chapter 10

The Realisations

I was struck by how welcoming my dad's friends were to Shyam. When my mother had shared with me that dad did joyfully extend his happiness to his friends that he's been spared from the traditional groom hunting - it was a silent approval. The warm words and lively pats my partner received from my father's friends merely wasn't a matter of courtesy but a respect to my dad's being, their friendship and obviously how beautifully dad could have possibly discussed Shyam.

The complicated ritual bore from my hands although Shyam not just being a mere spectator but a pillar of support. The warm reception of dad's favourite friends might have healed parts of Shyam, which sought forgiveness. We knew we were blessed enough to know that dad had approved of this relationship. In fact, mom told me that dad was happy. He knew Shyam was still seeking a job.

As per mom, dad broke all the conventional stigma of society when he assured that job would come in due time. I had gotten a job merely 20 days prior to my dad's death. But my dad's trust in me was immense that he was ready to discuss marriage with Shyam's family. His thoughts challenged conventional stereotypes. Among his generation, his level of open-mindedness felt exemplary. To him education and good character mainly mattered rather than societal expectations or material status. The profound sense of loss hit harder when I realised what I had truly lost.

He was to be placed above all conventional notions and stereotypes with his progressive perspectives. I realised how wrong I was when my picture about him was that of a typical father whose demands are ingrained in the deep minds surpassing generation to generation. His ideas made me realise that maybe to some parents it was an end of the era of stereotypical gender norms and surpassing of some the traditional boundaries. I found a treasure, too late and by the time I found it, he was gone. I silently pleaded for forgiveness, recognizing just how much he was to be held in high regard...

I realised mom did the right thing by revealing our relationship. Her timely intervention spared me from crushing guilt. At least he was aware of the truth. I felt immensely grateful for the gut feeling she had.

Are we all a little naive?

We see people, of course!

But what to do with this vision

that is unable to penetrate skin deep, bone deep?

That makes us carry scales,

in hopes of deciphering human waves of love,

to capture it when it crashes against our soul.

All the ages we carry scales,

only to realise the depth of love wave

when it recedes from our soul.

Part IV

Depression

Chapter 11

Zooming in Icy Landscapes

Weeks and months passed. The left side of my bookshelf bore a thicker layer of dust, it used to be dad's collection. Life felt unusually colourless as if it lost its essence. Mom seemed concerningly silent while making it hard to help me distinguish if it was a masquerade of courage or a genuine one. Through the initial weeks, she hardly went for a drive or a walk. Nothing excited her. It was hard for both of us to laugh or smile from within. It felt particularly difficult to maintain a facade of normalcy as if society was watching us. It might be a fallacy to believe that society demanded smiles or watched us keen. Once in a while when we used to go out, when necessary, we used to get sympathetic stares. Eventually I was tired of being under some imaginary tragic spotlight.

The certainty of irrevocable loss slowly crept into our minds. The initial days or even weeks were harder. Food seemed bland, nights felt longer with sleeplessness to accompany and we functioned mechanically just to survive. Suffering felt meaningless and in search of finding some meaning in my suffering, I clung on to my toxic workplace. Mom carried on with her daily chores with a false sense of forced rhythm. Grief is a very personal process and everyone does it differently. I often ponder if the intensity of sorrow felt heavier because we were bonded by a nuclear family. Something about grief felt inexplicable, it could be its nature which wasn't fully grasped yet.

The depression stage definitely has crying as its core response for the majority of them but it's not just that. We start to intellectually process and realise the loss and that hurts deep. We observe shades of the deceased person's personality that were sidelined while they were alive. The 4:00 a.m. kitchen seemed hauntingly silent without dad. It used to be both mom and dad clearing the kitchen tasks. Dad was the man of shared responsibilities. There were times where he used to do my laundry, iron and fold clothes for me. He would sweep and mop the floor during evenings and at times, mornings when mom had her tiring days. They both used to enthusiastically converse and cook together before he left for work. Acts of service was clearly his love language that he helped me guide what to seek in a partner or even fragments of how to be a partner.

With the good memories also came the ones we once wished to forget. However, I did not want it to fade as it was an honour to relive the memories understanding how imperfectly perfect, we fragile humans were. It was not just my father's memories which passed through but also my dear friend's whom I lost to covid. Yet, with all of these happening all at once - or even with single chest numbers systematically; the experience felt unfathomable. My mom and I often isolated ourselves from going out. Waking up to the realisation of the loss, the fading scent of dad and not hearing his voice felt like a daily routine of snooze-less alarms.

The realisation that there won't be new narratives struck hard. Their voices lingered on my mind like the audio recordings.

Their accent, slang, tonalities all play in a repeat mode. The gleam in my friend's eyes when something made him happy, the way he had complained about silly things, the way dad raised his eyebrows when in awe making his wrinkles more prominent, his serious expressions when deep in thought, his laughter - my mind tried remembering everything it could. I had episodes of anxiety attacks when the realisations settled in. My mind had difficulty navigating through intense emotions of the uncertainty if we will ever meet our loved ones who had departed, the feeling of betrayal of being left alone, the wreckage of not knowing how to survive without them. My whole life seemed to be blurring the line between fact and fiction. To pay the price of being survivors felt hard.

Chapter 12

Pervasiveness of Guilt

I found myself running away from something heavy and the shadows of it tried outrunning me. Guilt. Guilt barged in. In my psychology classes, I did learn that guilt was often accompanied with grief. I already had an insight of what was happening but the insight wasn't enough to navigate. To break down my part of guilt into two experiences; one was causational and the other was of my role.

When my dearest friend passed away to covid, it was May 2021. I had known about his death many days later through my friend who had checked his social media while I was panicking. To know more about it, weeks later I texted one of his friends on social media. I wanted to know about the parts of his story which led to his loss. I was told that he had travelled to his native place. It was the second wave of the covid pandemic and he passed away from COVID.

Some days prior to him travelling, we did have a phone conversation. He used to casually talk about his after-dinner walks which made me feel uneasy. I did warn him not to risk his health since the second wave planted seeds of panic and flashbacks among the survivors. He was careful, he was healthy but somewhere the miscalculations happened.

The 'role' guilt consumed me. I felt like I was not a good friend. I started to believe that I was the reason he didn't inform me about leaving for his native place for a small vacation. I felt guilty for not helping him with the last thing he had requested about. I collected his younger sister's number from this friend of his. I wasn't sure if she knew me. I did not know what to say or how to introduce myself. The uncertainty dragged my initial efforts. One fine day, the very sole thought of me identifying with his soul felt enough to begin with, but what if she ends up being angry at me for not reaching out any sooner? I was anxious.

I decided to make the call. We spoke. The conversation turned into opening our hearts. To my surprise, she sounded much more mature than her age. I did not know if it was the trauma or if she was different. I could sense the slight shift of sombre to some amount of peace. I wanted to meet her in-person and share my part of stories about her brother. The only thing that stopped me was guilt. What if I was actually a terrible friend? I decided to keep in touch with her through texts. Maybe in some months I might get the strength to meet her.

After months, I happened to visit my social media page. A message sent around May 2021 from a familiar name struck my eyes. It read, "Di (Elder sister), my brother passed away from COVID". It was a message from the same younger sister. She did try informing me but it was only after months I realised that his sister tried informing me but something delayed the entire passing of information. I believed in the divine timing of events. The question itself of why it was delayed despite attempts of letting me know lingered on my mind.

It wasn't just it. Guilt crept into my blood and bones differently. Along with the role guilt, the causational guilt revolved around my father's death. The guilt of what all I could have done to stop it. I was plagued with such thoughts. "If I would have forced him to take the right treatments maybe we could have prevented this." "If I were a little early to help him reach the hospital maybe he would have been alive." The role guilt amplified the suffering. My mind ached contemplating if I was a good daughter. I wandered alone in the whirl of ifs and no's. In short, I felt 1 ½ guilty of their deaths.

"Would it be a spiritual scandal to be expecting the births and not the deaths?

To some there must be an expectancy.

But to some, they are thrown off into the ocean while being asleep.

And if we were to have known a death date if our loved ones,

Would we act a bit kinder?

And if we act a bit kinder,

Is it love or an escape from our own feelings of guilt?

And if life was full of uncertainties,

Why are we wired for attachments?"

Chapter 13

Coldest Waves

The first part of the society felt kinder. Friends reached out; families reached out to check in. Some maintained consistency. My personal experience of despair was coldly silent. I did not let everyone open those shackles. To save my own peace, I only let a few of them in. I realised that even when the world shatters, even though grief is an ebb and flow; we only let the real ones comfort us. To the ones who had previously wronged me, I held no grudges. However, to protect my part of the grieving space, to honour my grieving journey, I respectfully chose to maintain a distance. I was open for conversations for the ones who were truly concerned and sincere.

My toxic workplace started taking a different toll on me. I used to stay day in and night finishing work tasks, the off days were covered too. Initially I chose to suffer only because the workplace suffering made sense. Later on, I clung on to the suffering with the sudden shift of responsibilities; financial responsibilities precisely. Life had entirely changed with no warnings. The empty spaces of my mind felt glaringly strenuous as if I am being judged, unable to shield it. The organisation witnessed mass resignation. With a bunch of coworkers resigning, the work felt too obnoxious. I clung onto the work hoping to endure a bit longer. The sense of responsibility grew day by day. The grief magnified.

The legal and personal parts were to be sorted and settled. Renaming and cancelling accounts and memberships became a part of secondary losses while reminding us of accepting what we had lost. Closing of the bank account was a part of it. It felt heavy because dad was my companion mostly whenever I visited the bank. Not having him besides and answering the officials about his absence was harder. There were people who were still unaware about dad's death and restating the narratives felt like re-living the pain for both me and mom. Some couldn't believe while some expressed sadness that they couldn't attend the funeral.

Mom took responsibility for reminding me of sorting out dad's personal belongings but her efforts were futile. Donating, reusing and organising were parts of navigating loss in a better way. But I wasn't ready to confront the finality yet.

My wardrobe had a wine colour maxi gown of mine. It was lastly ironed by dad and it lied suspended on the hanger. I did not touch it. I did not want to alter its position; every little crease had the warmth of my dad's touch. But when it came to dad's clothes, it was the scent that lingered and memory that was woven. There were times when I would cling to his shirt and weep. I had no idea that his belongings would carry such emotional weight. It had his imprints and I wasn't ready to let it go.

Almost every son or daughter wishes to express their gratitude towards their parents with their first salary. I was among them too. But how does it feel to have received a prorated payment since you had joined mid-month and you only realise that a few days after your dad's death? I could never share the joy of receiving a pay from a full-time job although I had gifted him things out of the pocket money. I faced a grim fate when I had missed the notification of my pay while my dad was alive.

I started withdrawing. I started sticking only to the bare essentials. Every single chore felt extra draining. I spent time watching my dad's favourite shows, songs and reading books. The shared experiences made me miss my loved ones even more. The sense to connect with them rose with every moment that resonated.

My memories poured in. I missed the way he used to hold my hands while crossing the road. I missed the way I rushed towards the door around 6:00 p.m. when the doorbell rang because checking the snacks he bought for me was a part of a tireless child-like routine. I missed the way he used to oil my hair and apply aloe vera on it. Despite years of experience, he failed at tying me a ponytail. And after every hair care session, I used to tease him with the same effortless joke to at least try tying me one. I recalled the way he broke into laughter while trying and after a few failed attempts handing over the task to mom. Dad would peel pomegranates for me, each bowl full of love! It wasn't just pomegranate but every single fruit I have eaten. But when it was pomegranate, his ruby stained hands spoke volumes of love! Back then it was only one of the regular days; now a prominent memory. It was hard.

I also realised that my birthdays won't ever be the same. Dad knew how much I loved balloons and he made sure to decorate our home with those. Every single time, he celebrated it, making me feel like a little princess. It brought me back to another incident.

Years ago, when I was just around one or two as per mom, I travelled to my hometown with my mom. Dad was in Mumbai, working without having received long leave. What does a 1 or 2-year-old know about her 'Papa'? I was told that I called out 'Papa' with my little voice while searching for him beneath the table, the chair, the leaves, the flowers, and all the places my little hands could reach. I went around calling out Papa at every possible nook and corner. Grandma felt deeply moved that she asked mom never to carry me to our hometown without my dad. It was evident that the word 'Papa' wasn't attached to a father figure but a concept of comfort and security. I slowly realised that my 1- or 2-year-old self knew that Papa meant love and the longing was expressed in the most unexpected way.

Now that I have lost him, I feel as if I've lost every abstract aspect that the child in me had once connected with. I started writing down my thoughts and emotions in hopes of finding new meanings to my suffering. Most pages had a common theme; how bleak life was without them.

A few months passed and my mental health started deteriorating due to work pressure. On seeing me struggle, my mom and Shyam motivated me to quit. The validation felt stronger as already I was coping through multiple things. I felt heard and affirmed that my health was being prioritised. I quit from the toxic workplace. It felt much lighter but the financial responsibility kept haunting me. I was in search of a new job.

In the midst of it all, I was careful to compartmentalise my grieving journey from my relationship. In simple words, I did not want my grieving journey to affect my partner or the relationship.

The goal was not to be opaque about my grief. I was transparent enough. The goal was to find the right balance. He was definitely a part of my grieving journey. It wasn't just my loss. He lost a friend, a father-in-law who could have resonated with him and supported his dreams. But since that attachment was not made, the grief would have been entirely different for him.

There were times when I needed support and he used to patiently listen to my memories, my stories and my emotional breakdowns. I felt grateful for every single time he had supported me despite his own struggles. A few friends of mine believed that my love relationship could fill the void left by my dad's death. A companion, a friend or any kind person could be a solace during difficult times. But grief is often misunderstood and only the griever knows the depth of its pain. It must not be a presumption to outstate that nobody in this whole world could fill in the void. There's nothing equivalent in this whole world that might replace a bond.

Months passed. Being unable to provide invoked feelings of helplessness. My nights were filled with self-sabotaging thoughts while days were shrouded by hope. The feelings of despair were bound to happen with a plethora of happenings but surrendering wasn't a choice. I had my obligations which sustained my motivation to pursue job opportunities. Though I strived for a job, I was clear that I wanted to work from home. I wanted my physical presence to comfort mom during her grieving process. Her grief was profound as she had lost her partner and a companion. To let her grieve alone would augment her battle. This was my choice beyond all obligations.

Having endured struggles, I secured a job. A part of the financial struggle died within me. With every death something alters, paving paths to new beginnings and new reality. The new place brought fresh hopes. New people, new circle and new hopes. The new workplace had a supportive work culture, making me realise the impact of workplaces in our lives. A new found peace among the chaos embraced me.

Part V

Acceptance

Chapter 14

Pondering Over the Melting Ice-berg

The second part of the society felt strikingly beautiful. It was the realisation that some connections are beyond time. Some people carry glimmers projecting kindness and providing a safe space. They make way for self-growth and revitalise our half-dead selves.

Lubna was one of them. The person who helped me identify a part of me which was stronger than I expected. One of the most beautiful qualities about someone is the awareness of what we want and what we don't. She was beautifully aware of that. She made me realise that it shouldn't take extreme struggles or abuse to learn to say no. One of the most powerful qualities! She was the one who wanted me to stop entertaining people that bred toxicity. The uncomfort itself should be the prime reason for self-advocacy. We both knew that it need not be applicable in every single situation. She always wanted me to put myself first.

Constructive criticism and condescension have a fine line. I have known people who use condescension in disguise of constructive criticism. The composing we force ourselves before conversing with the condescending ones is futile with the extent our soul drains and diminishes. Lubna was that fine line. She was the grace that helped me notice the difference.

Lubna would open up her stories, her struggles and views on life. While my part of melancholic stories hardly was relatable to her - as she would readily admit, she always made sure to validate my pain. The mere assurance that bigger experiences are on the way and life has its own way of unravelling gave me hopes. The beauty was, she couldn't relate much of it but she could understand. When the reassurance overflowed despite her own struggles; her truth and charm set me new hopes.

I found another bond, Alex. Again, someone who could see through my soul effortlessly. He often said he had no idea how he would have handled a situation like that of mine. But I knew he would have managed it well; he had a knack of reading unspoken pain. He would say, "Why wouldn't you feel overwhelmed and lost? You are doing everything all at once, just like someone twice your age." It felt funny but was a poignant metaphor. My unseen struggles felt visible with his words of affirmation.

Once I was in tears, remembering my father, when a video suddenly popped up on my phone. It was a recording of Alex singing a song steeped in themes of dad-daughter love. The timing felt magically aligned, as if my dad was reaching out to console me. It was the same song I once found grating because dad would listen to that on repeat. But since his passing, it is one of my favourites. With a light heart I can admit that maybe he hasn't changed at all, he chose the same song to console me. The sign I got synced with the sense of connection I desperately needed with my dad.

I didn't hesitate to share how thankful I was. I knew he wouldn't mock me. He would patiently listen and then share his thoughts. He often told me that I was strong, his words adorned my resilience. He saw things differently, probably an empath. He knew what grief was. It felt effortless for me to share my pain, since he was a person of depth; a switch between absurdism and existentialism covered up in kindness.

Both Lubna and Alex are the emotional support we all need during our darkest hours.

With all of this happening, I realised that I started seeing things differently. The lens of grief had a different shade. The shift from remembering my dad with pain to cherishing his memories wasn't a one-day process but eventually I was there!

All of these people had a share to help me see things differently. Maybe it was they who helped me, giving me the space to open up about my pain. Their ears tirelessly listened to my stories; their fingers wiped away my tears. It wasn't just Lubna or Alex; Neha's support was a constant reassurance. I never realised Jyoti could comfort me from miles away. My partner has been a constant support; providing me the time, space and affection to heal my open wound. My mother, who shared a grief journey with me, is my strongest pillar of strength. Her determination and resilience had a radiant grace. I trusted my sorrows and pain with these people since they were the safe space and it was the right decision!

For the ones who were intentionally or unknowingly rude, I chose to forgive. It might be the lack of empathy, insecurity or ungratefulness. It definitely tells us more about their unhealed parts or unresolved issues. I learnt to respectfully keep my distance from them. As mentioned earlier, I needed to honour my part of the grief journey.

For the people who were clueless not knowing how to handle the situation or how to console a grieving person, who did not show up when needed, grief might be a new experience to them. It could have been a situation where they were anxious of saying the wrong words, doing the wrong things or even not knowing what to do. It could be that they were finding it difficult to navigate sensitive emotions. It might also be true that they might have not yet grasped the depth of loss.

I gained some insights on the complexities of emotions and human nature after my dad's death. It is often said that we realise more about our bonds and connections during such crucial events of our lives. To have a support system is important. Not just the validation or reassurance, the new perspectives we gain from them change the outlook on death.

One such insight I had gained and gotten reassured was that our loved ones that passed away find ways to watch, protect and comfort us. It could be the little signs we see, the mannerisms or phrases we notice in somebody else that our loved ones used to exhibit in the past, their favourite scent, song or even a text message at the times we find ourselves sunk in tears!

I have learnt that we have people of our kind to whom we connect with, making grief a shared human experience. The collective wisdom and solace make us hold on to them. In the quietest moments we realise that our grief feels less heavy with them in our lives. It's the trust that assures us we are embraced by safe arms.

Chapter 15

Blooming into Understanding Guilt

I was in a supervision session with one of my supervisors. I told her that I felt guilty about certain things that revolved around my grief journey. The first thing I was told to do was to acknowledge the grief feelings as it is before introspecting even if it didn't mean that I should actually feel guilty. I knew that it was natural to feel guilty while grieving. But with my supervisor, I found a way to reflect on these feelings and navigate the emotions.

The role guilt and causational guilt I had was addressed. I was asked if I could predict the future and even if I could, would I have been able to save them from the grips of death. She used a metaphor to help me with the process. She told me that life is like a train journey. We meet people, sometimes we bond, some people we avoid. She asked me if it was absolutely necessary that the ones we bond with, all get down with me at the same destination. I remained silent. She asked me to visualise all kinds of approaches to stop them from getting down to their destination; anger, bargaining, love, anything to prevent them from getting off to their intended stop. She asked me that, even if I prevent them from getting off their destination, how long I could actually make them stay. She gave me space to reflect.

I couldn't. The reflection that I couldn't predict the future or any other factors that might have caused death lingered. Understanding death as an inevitable part of life made things meaningful. Whatever is meant to happen will happen whenever it is supposed to, we can appreciate the journey they had with us rather than fixating on destinations.

Even if I did all the pending tasks I was expected to, even if I was imperfectly perfect throughout my roles as a daughter or a friend, their death would still be inevitable. She emphasised that the single thing I kept pending might not actually mean that I wasn't a good friend or overshadow the good moments we had shared together.

Not everyone witnesses all milestones being achieved, which raises the question of whether we can truly rely on the idea that someone left without experiencing certain moments. Certainly, the numbers may rise and fall in comparison, but what precisely are we comparing?

I was not in control of these things. She told me to take responsibility if some parts of guilt felt rational. It still remains a question as I am still grieving and it's not a mandate that I have to find an answer. I can still choose to work on my guilt from the experience I have learnt. The entire conversation with my supervisor (a psychologist, REBT practitioner) helped me navigate feelings of guilt in a healthier way. Seeking therapy during such crucial transitions play an important role in our further lives. Professional help would definitely help us gain fresher insights and a direction about how to self-explore.

Chapter 16

Acting upon Guilt

Now, the question was - what actions might help me feel better about this? I wrote down letters and short messages to them. I penned down the shared memories, the untold stories and the favourites they gave me. Inking down my thoughts and emotions helped me process grief better. Sometimes I would explore responses the way they would have if they were to be alive. A part of me felt less isolated. The cathartic process released much of the emotional weight, making me feel heard and understood.

Journaling was an explorational choice to bid the departed ones goodbye. Since we humans don't have a map to grieve or checklists to do while grieving, it was my personal choice to revisit connections the way I wanted. Eventually I realised that I wasn't looking for closure. The word closure might have various interpretations and personal perspectives attached but for me the finality of an emotional, mental and spiritual goodbye remains a question mark.

I understand that the final goodbye need not mean that everyone and everything once we bonded with are severed. When sorrows meet hopes and despair meets love; the grief would definitely meet remembrance. To me, the word final goodbye is attached to a physical departure. Our loved ones live within us even though we accept their death and our loss. We have their cherished memories and traces of love, light and their essence.

I made a folder of their photographs separately making it a dedicated space. My mom and I sorted out the personal belongings, some to be donated while some kept for reusing. Items intended to be disposals were disposed off. Belongings which held sentimental value even as simple as a pen were decided to be kept. We did not want to rush in. We were sure that maybe someday we will revisit the items as the process definitely felt heavily overwhelming but a powerful step towards acceptance.

With an overwhelming heart, I decided to meet my friend's home. It was a difficult step. The moment I stepped in, welled up eyes looked at me. It was his mother. She cried her heart out. My grip tightened but I felt that no amount of strength in this whole world could carry the weight of her loss. I could feel the pain of a mother penetrating through my chest! I cried too! My fragile self couldn't hold her ocean of emotions. We sought solace in each other for that one human, her son. How powerful it felt to have sensed such enormous love. Her ocean of emotions was nothing but immeasurable love towards her son.

I looked at his little sister Ammu. Her eyes reflected her shattered heart, a soul full of pain and a body that lost half a piece of her own self. She was the sibling who was brought to Earth by his request, I recollected a part of his story. He had once told me that he had always felt the need of having a sibling in case he was in need of heaven. My heart filled with overwhelming emotions.

My mom held space for his mother offering quiet comfort. Me and his sister moved into the room. We shared our memories. I could see a part of her ears' never-ending tiredness whenever I talked about her brother. I knew she was collecting all parts of her brother's unknown stories. Every part might have felt precious, and newer parts might have given little rebirths to his memories. That space I had was the most precious one I ever had in my life. Two humans, meeting for the first time sharing a deep existence that would live through our hearts, memories and stories!

Four differently grieving strong women under a roof bonded for a moment. The fierceness within our hearts held a silent promise to tirelessly carry parts of our loved ones throughout our lives. My guilt subdued; life humbled me more. I knew, if he was watching, he might have definitely echoed back the love. Like his mother said, he was too innocent to be upset with anyone and as far as I know, too loving to light up the darkest corners!

I am sorry for not sending the lifeboats.

I did not see this coming; I overlooked that anyone could leave anytime.

And even if I could,

You know how powerless I am.

The only power I have is to keep on loving you.

I'll remember you when the pansies bloom,

When I savour the sweet-sour passion fruit.

I'll remember the days when your joy met gloom

And how we shared our second thoughts

Without even knowing what hesitation was.

I'll write down the letters and keep the unsent postcards with me;

For, I don't know the addresses where it doesn't exist in our realms.

I'll cherish every single word I write for you.

The wind blows a bit different in here,

But I'll eagerly wait to tell you the happenings -

If it's the breezing cold or pouring rain

If it's the scorching sun or the 3:00 a.m. pain.

For I'll remember you like the last line of my favourite poem,

And every time I remember you, I'll help you break the immortality code.

Chapter 17

Reflecting Loss with the New Lens

Loss is one of the greatest transitions one can have in their life. It still remains a question of where one goes after death. What if they are beyond our five senses of sensation? What if they have found some other dimension which we have never been able to decipher? We all have personal interpretations about death that often resonate with cultural, spiritual and poetic expressions. The souls leave their physical body on Earth transiting some other journey. Maybe, the wise devised mortality for the earth to flourish and sustain the balance. If immortality on Earth was certain, the resources would have been exhausted, opportunities overlooked and all of us would have been stuck in the ceaseless loop of suffering. When the wise decide 'what and why', ledgers decide when and how. We negligible humans have never advanced to look beyond the permitted threshold. If we view death through a practical lens, death is a reflection of balance and sacrifice.

Some scriptures suggest that we all have signed up contracts and are playing our parts, so it would be evident that when the part gets over, the performer leaves. So, if the performer leaves, do we lose what we got to experience? We don't lose it; we miss some of it.

We miss parts of the performer. We carry some parts on our head, some on our hearts and some on our blood and bones. If their personal objects can hold a sentimental value, imagine the power of their identity we have carried all along!

The Shradh was a step towards learning acceptance. The wisdom passed over centuries reminds us that death is inevitable but love transcends. When the living legacies prayed and bowed for the ancestor of whom we have never seen, touched or heard of before, we formed a bridge closing the gap. It's an acknowledgement of the departed souls marking the transcending love. We obviously turn through the pages of known memories but when we pray for the ancestors, we also get to acknowledge the sequels of the unseen pages.

We seek forgiveness for the unknown and known mistakes made and the hope we are free from the guilt and have been forgiven is also a step towards acceptance. Grief, to some might also be a spiritual along with the intellectual process. It's a realisation that we are not just physical beings but something beyond though we were on earth for only a brief time. As per some beliefs, the departed souls might be in a different realm but we - the descendants get to offer gratitude and pass on the very core message that our loved ones remained to love through our stories, rituals, memories and that the bridge of love only goes longer!

The rituals, the activities we redo, the letters we write and the responses we write back from their perspective is all an attempt to comprehend the play of dichotomy. Life and death are intricately woven from the same source of thread. Every death gives life a new set of realisations and in the quest of grieving journey, we seek the meaning of life; something which is deeply personal. We humble down realising that all of this is a part of temporary existence and fragility. In the attempt, we often submit to acceptance knowing or unknowingly. But is it true that grief always ends up in acceptance? Has grief been a linear journey? Why is it difficult to confront conversations about mortality when death is an ultimate truth?

Chapter 18

Talking about The 'Iceberg' in the Room

Conversations about death have always been daunting. In some cultures, it is even a taboo to talk about death. Some refrain from engaging in such conversations because the concept of death can be triggering, making death a common discomfort. I personally feel and back the notion that discussing death would encourage us to reflect about life and its sensitive nature.

What could be more meaningful than discussing the abstracts of life? There have been people who have the insight that discussing death is a part of the platter. However, I've noticed that some often forget the sensitivity that comes along with the concept of death. I've overheard a conversation a daughter had with her parents, she said, "When you both die, I will be the only person looking after the closed ones". The words sounded like they were moreover task oriented like a sense of obligation which definitely might have not been the case, it could have been an attempt to state out the reassurance. However, the tone lacked its sensitivity. It almost sounded like a burden of responsibilities rather than a commitment. Of course, it shouldn't have sounded like throwing a fish in the tank especially when the parents are older. Humans deserve more of the emotional connection and gentleness when engaged in such conversations.

I attempted to weigh my approach about sensitivity during such discussions. I was told that everyone is going to die someday so there's no harm in stating it openly as a truth. I partially agreed with the former fact. I had to deny the perspectives of what the truth of 'death-talk' meant to both of us.

We all are different individuals with different levels of sensitivities. Death is an ultimate truth, but the space we speak about death must feel safe. Our goal is not to create a sense of fear and anxiety. A bit of kindness, compassion and the right choice of words can make the space feel safer. What humans feel over such conversations might be subjective but how we put in the words can either leave scars of fear or imprints of compassion. The truth is inevitable but the experience and feelings associated needs to be honoured. How beautiful it must be to discuss death and grief in a gentle way?

Death is not always suffering. To some it might be the end of their agonies while to some, it might be a mortgage-free acceptance. Every person holds their own perception about death but all of us strive for the human connection. It's a beautiful delight that we get to meet people in our lifetimes and it's an expansion of love when we carry over the kindness while talking about departures.

Chapter 19

Shifting Spring; Yet Nurturing

Is it true that grief always ends up in acceptance? Almost a year and half after a young son's death, I visited his mother. The eyes still sunken, meals hardly touched and trembles at the thought of her son. I realised this was prolonged grief. She has lost appetite, somehow manages to perform daily routines including household chores but hesitates to go outside. It was understandable since her son was her travel companion. Every place she visited with him might have been associated with a core memory. "Sometimes, I look out of the window, in case he returns", the words spoke of her daily battles.

I was told that some of her acquaintances had given her hopes that her son will be back soon someday. I was unsure if they were being dismissive of her pain or confused about the right words in the process of consoling her. The false assertions gave her nothing but unrealistic expectations. For me, it sounded like cruelty rather than compassion. With such false narratives they hinder her journey towards acceptance paving the path towards prolonged pain. I agree that not everyone might have the bandwidth to offer support to a grieving person but certain misconceptions or superficial conversations about death, knowingly put forward by the society can make the griever feel disconnected from reality.

I recollected a two-decade old grief story told by my mom a long time ago. I asked her for more clarity. It was about a mother who had lost her son in an accident. The mother took her son to her hometown without his wishes and tragically he passed away in an accident. Feelings of guilt carved into the mother's heart. The mother starved with a broken heart and sadly she passed away a few weeks later. It must have been gut wrenching for that mother. Grief can also be life threatening if we miss on the crucial signs of when to seek help!

There might be a lot of other factors where a person is unable to achieve acceptance. Acceptance is not the horizon but finding a path to navigate through the pain and attempting to heal for ourselves, our loved ones and the departed ones is integral. The right place to seek help would be to go to a mental health professional. Grief may not always lead to acceptance. It's a personal journey. Therapy would not make grief magically disappear but the suffering would find new insights and the attempt to process the pain will find healthier frameworks.

Humans are designed to seek connection and being involved in a support group would make the grievers feel heard. Support groups have a powerful impact when it comes to grief journeys! As stated earlier every single person grieves differently. However, there might be some commonalities that when heard makes the listener feel less isolated. The feeling that we aren't stranded and there are people somewhere with some other similar or different experiences creates a safe and familiar space. The griever need not have to worry about the emotional bandwidth of the listener because the doors of support groups are heavily welcoming for shared stories and support. Every follow up provides strength for healing and new found hopes to grieve openly. Support groups and therapy act as a light during such darkest times of our lives.

Chapter 20

Is Grief Linear?

The five stages of grief have been a model given by Elisabeth Kubler-Ross. It helps as a framework to understand the grieving process. The stages are denial, anger, bargaining, depression and acceptance. It is a reality that grief is not linear and we don't process grief in a structured manner. However, this framework helps us a lot to navigate and identify emotions. It is true that there happens to be revisits of the stages.

Grief is like waves. One moment we are fine, sitting in a chair and listening to random songs and suddenly a favourite song of our departed loved one plays, releasing a flood of memories unleashing the bargaining part of ourselves despite having touched acceptance. Even in moments of acceptance, despair can still creep in, like a glimpse through the parted curtain of the window sill. There are feelings of anger when the chaos of life storms up or when it feels unfair to bear so much pain despite having a sense of acceptance. Grief has never been linear for me nor the stages acted up independently. It felt like they co-existed.

The framework holds huge value to have drawn out some findings. However, there is no correct order or way to grieve.

Everybody's path is different. Even two people grieving over a single human is different; the stages might be different; the emotions might be different and experiences would also be different. Human complexities are beyond our comprehension. The waves of grief revisit. Which wave hits us decides on how to sail. It would definitely be unpredictable but the course can be adjusted!

Chapter 21

The Little Warmth of Spring

"This shall too pass" is often a phrase some of us use during the hardest times of our lives. When my dad passed away, Shyam visited and wrote this in one of my notepads. Reflecting on the words now, it is evident that nothing is permanent. The joy, pain, suffering, hardships, setbacks, happiness - nothing! After leaving a toxic workplace, I found another wonderful place. Shyam got placed with a job and mom revived her cooking channel, and my friend who also lost her dad, is now successfully running her dad's business. Each of these experiences reminds me that nothing is constant.

The waves would be back, the winter will also be! As much as I understand grief is a unique journey, our minds might revisit the stages. We have to identify, acknowledge and choose to take action. It could be revisiting our loved ones' activities, writing them a letter, support groups or even holding on to the spiritual rituals of remembrance.

To be someone's child, parent, partner, sibling, friend- it's an honour. It's an honour to be somebody's someone. It isn't much different in the case of pets who were companions. Even the slightest of love you provided to the cat you saw while the morning walk or the biscuits you fed some street dog; every single thing counts. As long as we are here, the legacy will continue! The bygone souls would realise that our hearts are capable of cradling their essence, minds designed to replay them and eyes would soften up with teary lullabies of slumber. When our love transcends it opens up new doors of possibilities.

I am yet to realise what I am made up of!

Is it just blood, bones, skin and hormones?

Or something beyond?

Am I an embodiment of words?

Or another ignorant existence?

Do I have that particle of the first atom?

A pinch of some stars? Or just the dust?

And how about the conscience?

The consciousness or nothingness?

Is it my first time on this earth?

Or my millionth birth?

Where would I go from here?

Back to the one who sent me?

Or to a new womb I owe thee?

Acknowledgements

A number of people helped me through my grieving and writing journey and I am more than grateful for their support. I would like to sincerely thank you all for even the slightest of efforts for your kindness, and consistent support!

To my dear mother, Prasanna Yesodharan, you have been my constant support throughout my life. This book would have never been possible without you! You noticed my creative writings from my very younger age and affirmed me to be a writer. It all started with the pen you gifted me! You are my strength and the sacrifices you made for me is what I am today. Your kindness is contagious. I hope you realise how powerful and beautiful you are!

To my dear father, Yesodharan K, who is no longer with us… You have been my constant light throughout. I realised that you were my greatest supporter who trusted my decisions. You taught me to be resilient. I have a gift of seeing things in depth and lately I realised that it was an inherited lens of vision from you. It was you all the time! Your taste in music, books, your personal narratives and perspectives shaped my lens to view life. I'll be carrying this gift all along!

To my fiancé, Shyam S Nair. Thank you for your constant love and belief in me. You are my favourite person to share life's ups and downs and it is my greatest joy. I appreciate how you support my dreams and it means the world to me! I am grateful to have you as my companion. Blessed to have you in my life!

To my soul brother, Vishnu. Thank you for being there for me. I feel blessed to have known a kind, strong and beautiful soul. I know you are still there, cheering me in every way you can.

To my soul sister, Jyoti Laguri. Thank you for being my constant. You are the sweetest woman I've known and your belief in me keeps me going! You've been the kindest person throughout and my safest story keeper. Inexplicably, you fill some void of my life!

To my soul sister, Sneha Ganesh. Thank you for being my constant power. Your honesty and determination have always inspired me! You have always been there, lifting me up and you truly are a rare gem! You belong to my heart!

To my soul sister, Lubna Riaz. Thank you for being an honest and powerful lady. You've pushed me to be my best and you gave me hopes when I had second thoughts about myself. Thank you for reminding me that every page is worth writing, I am aware that I can always count on you!

To my to-be-sister-in-law, Drishya Dileep. Thank you for being a constant friend for more than a decade. Your presence in my life changed my life in a beautiful way. I'll always be grateful to have you!

To my soul friend, Alex Edward. The tireless efforts to listen to my stories has meant more to me than words can ever express. Thank you for holding space for my struggles and reassuring me when I needed it the most. You've been like family and I am grateful for the deep understanding we hold!

Thank you, Vishnupriya Nair, for being a beautiful soul, you are my dearest little sister of all! Thank you Sreejith, my cousin brother, for being a support during my hard times.

Infinitely grateful to Smt. Chinmoyee Chakraborty, my English teacher during school who identified my literary talents and encouraged me to bring out my best. Your motherly affection still lingers in my heart! Deep gratitude for Mr Joseph, my teacher who made me realise how impartial and fair a teacher should be!

Deep gratitude to my friends who've been a constant support through decades. Thank you Shebin Varghese, Sreelakshmi Anand, Chithra Iyer and Mithun Achari. Thank you, Sneha Patteri, for the love you have always had for me.

Truly grateful to my to-be-in-laws, Mr Sivaprasad and Mrs Radhika for the random check-in calls and reassurances.

Heartfelt thanks to Kalyani Joshi for being the lady who kept reminding me of my worth with your kindness and random glimmers.

I feel enormously thankful for the safe space I've found among some truly remarkable individuals– Aadithya Nath, Nazima Sayyed, Aarathi Bhaskaran, Sanjana Buravalla, Jitesh Madahar and Aishwarya Vora. Thank you, Taha Zaidi for providing me a little space in your safe circle which helped me cope with grief effectively! Grateful to Aashika Samuel for her encouraging words about my writing, expressing that she would be among those to buy my book if I ever published! The words meant a lot to me! Grateful for have experienced how miraculously beautiful Smt. Nithya Rao's heart is!

Thanks a lot for this Notion Press publishing house for giving me the space to express myself. Sincere gratitude to Charmine Joseph, assistant manager (sales) for being supportive during my writing journey, providing the strength and motivation. Sincere gratitude to Rashiga Gajendiran, Pre-Publishing Manager for all the support throughout.

Heartfelt gratitude to Jewel John, publishing manager for being a constant point of contact. Your patience and commitment has helped me throughout this journey.

Immensely grateful to my ancestors for providing me the inner strength to face the world!

Thanks to my city – Mumbai; for the dreams you had placed me in my heart and held my hands to create an impact!

www.ingramcontent.com/pod-product-compliance
Lightning Source LLC
LaVergne TN
LVHW040948150826

845672LV00002B/585
9798895889756